THE ELECTRIFYING SILENT SURGE

How the Electric Car Revolution Fuels Inflation

A ROBERT BONNER, JR Book

AUTHOR'S NOTE

This story is a work of fiction, inspired by real economic principles and peer-reviewed research. The characters and events are purely fictional, any resemblance to real persons or events are coincidental. The references used in this story are also fictional and created for illustrative purposes.

All rights reserved. No part of this book, THE ELECTRIFYING SILENT SURGE: How the Electric Car Revolution Fuels Inflation, may be reproduced, distributed, or transmitted in any form or by any means, including photocopying, recording, or other electronic or mechanical methods, without the prior written permission of the author, except in the case of brief quotations for the purpose of referring the book.

For permissions requests, contact:

People Will Read Again Book Publishing

Copyright 2024, © A Robert Bonner, Jr Book

1º Edition, "THE ELECTRIFYING SILENT SURGE How the Electric Car Revolution Fuels Inflation"

TABLE OF CONTENTS

INTRODUCTION
CHAPTER 1: **4**
   THE RISING POPULARITY OF ELECTRIC CARS 4
CHAPTER 2: **10**
   ECONOMIC PRINCIPLES AND INFLATION 10
      How Different Sectors Contribute to Inflation 13
      The Role of Technological Advancements in Economic Shifts 19
CHAPTER 3: **26**
   CASE STUDIES 26
CHAPTER 4: **41**
   THE PSYCHOLOGICAL AND SOCIAL IMPACT 41
      Social Dynamics in Electric Vehicle Adoption 51
CHAPTER 5: **58**
   POLICY AND REGULATION 58
      Incentives and Economic Consequences for Inflation 64
CHAPTER 6: **73**
   POLICY AND ECONOMIC OUTCOMES 73
      Studies Linking Policy Changes to Economic Outcomes 73
CONCLUSION **85**
      The Way Forward 87
      Final Thoughts and Call to Action 88

INTRODUCTION

In the last couple of decades, electric cars have been hailed as the giant leap toward a cleaner, greener future (Dearing, 2023)[1].

Governments and environmental groups alike have joined in a very vocal chorus, touting this switch from gas-fueled to electric-powered cars, promising reduced emission flows and a much smaller carbon footprint (Andersen & Wolsink, 2021)[2].

Sleek, silent EVs increasingly flood streets across the globe, their quiet hum heralding a new age for personal transportation.

However, at the heart of this green revolution lies an unforeseen economic consequence-inflation. Behind this veil of technological advancement, a silent surge has begun to affect the economy in ways few have foreseen.

The global rush into electric vehicles has inadvertently sparked inflationary pressures that are hitting industries, consumers, and whole nations. The intuitive answer, of course, is counterintuitive.

Electric cars are supposed to save money on fuel, reduce maintenance costs, and most of all, help stabilize the energy markets by lessening the dependence on oil (Rapson & Muehlegger, 2021)[3]. How is it that a technology designed to improve the world leads to rising prices for goods and services?

The answer lies in the economic ripple from this rapid transition: sky-socketing demand for key materials such as lithium and cobalt, supply chain strain, and huge investments in new energy infrastructure have all helped nudge the inflationary tide higher.

The EV supply chain is complex (Llamas-Orozco et al., 2023)[4]; adding to that layer the incentives and subsidies provided by governments have created a paradox whereby, while encouraging a cleaner environment, heavy economic consequences are imposed.

Understanding this relationship is not only important for economists and policymakers but also for consumers and businesses. The rise of electric vehicles affects everyone, whether you are a car owner, a taxpayer, or the buyer of everyday goods. Inflation, contributed by the electric car revolution, seeps into many facets of life-from the price of electronics to the cost of groceries.

And it's not just happening in one part of the world; this is a global phenomenon (Rapson & Muehlegger, 2021)[5].

Throughout this book, we will see how electric vehicles, though indubitably much 'cleaner' than their forebears, have at present, become an inflationary force. We shall break down the minutest details in the EV market, analyze the economic paradigms that drive inflation, and get a little close and personal with real-life case studies from leading electric car-adopting countries worldwide.

Along the way, we discuss the psychological and social impacts brought about by this transition, the role of government policies, and what the future holds as the world continues on this electrifying journey.

By the end of this journey, you'll have a clearer understanding of the economic forces at play, and more importantly, you'll see why addressing inflation concerns is essential for ensuring that the electric car revolution delivers on its promise without unintended economic fallout.

This article discusses how electric vehicles (EVs) are positioned as a significant part of policies aimed at reducing carbon emissions and achieving a cleaner, greener future [1].
1: Morgan, J. (2020). Electric vehicles: The future we made and the problem of unmaking it. Cambridge Journal of Economics, 44(4), 953-977. https://doi.org/10.1093/cje/beaa022

This article discusses how electric vehicles (EVs) are positioned as a central element to addressing major environmental, transportation and energy policy challenges[2].
2: Andersen, M. S., & Wolsink, M. (2021). Climate policy conflict in the U.S. states: A critical review and way forward. Climatic Change, 165(3), 1-19. https://doi.org/10.1007/s10584-022-03319-w

This paper discusses the economic rationale and policy implications of electric vehicles[3].
3: Rapson, D. S., & Muehlegger, E. (2021). The economics of electric vehicles. National Bureau of Economic Research Working Paper No. 29093. National Bureau of Economic Research. https://doi.org/10.3386/w29093

This article analyzes the logistics of lithium-ion batteries' global supply chain environmental impacts[4].
4: Llamas-Orozco, J. A., Meng, F., Walker, G. S., Abdul-Manan, A. F., MacLean, H. L., Posen, I. D., & McKechnie, J. (2023). Estimating the environmental impacts of global lithium-ion battery supply chain: A temporal, geographical, and technological perspective. PNAS Nexus, 2(11), pgad361. https://doi.org/10.1093/pnasnexus/pgad361

This paper further examines how EVs are contributing to global inflation[5]
5. Rapson, D. S., & Muehlegger, E. (2021). The economics of electric vehicles. National Bureau of Economic Research Working Paper No. 29093. National Bureau of Economic Research. https://doi.org/10.3386/w29093

CHAPTER 1:

THE RISING POPULARITY OF ELECTRIC CARS

Once upon a time in America, there existed a noisy internal combustion-dominated and incessantly smokey world of gasoline-fueled vehicles. Then in December 2010, the launch of the first mass-market electric vehicle, the Nissan Leaf brought in a definite interest and others like it soon followed, ushering in a quiet revolution that started to take shape.

This, in brief, was the beginning of an electric car era that would reboot transportation, reshape economies, and create a thick impasto of change in our daily life. Coming as they did, electric vehicles' impact was nothing short of transformational, changing not only the way we travel but even the texture of our economy.

During the latter part of the 19th century, old clunky steam-powered vehicles started giving way to superior combustion engines. It was during this time of technological change that a small but significant spark was struck in the imagination of inventors and entrepreneurs.

What had once been a sci-fi curiosity, the electric car was now starting to emerge as a formidable contender in the race for automotive superiority.

In the early 1900s, visionaries such as Ferdinand Porsche and Thomas Edison experimented with the first electric vehicle models (U.S. Department of Energy, 2014)[1]. Though novel, these designers would not go beyond prototype stages toward mass production and market sale.

With the modern electric car's silent ride and smooth acceleration, this was quite the contrast to the noisier, shaking combustion engine alternatives. Yet, the world was not quite ready to embrace this silent chariot fully, as the internal combustion engine and its promises of speed and range continued to sweep the stage of the automotive industry.

Now, use your imagination if you will... in 1897 there's a little inventor, Nikola Tesla, whom for decades was tormented by a dream of the car powered by electricity and not petrol.

This vision considered eccentric in his time started turning into reality at the beginning of the 21st century, just like the mystical mechanical clock, electric cars showed their potential to the world and promised to bring in a new era of clean and efficient transportation.

At first, these electric marvels were seen as a little more than fascinating mimickers of sci-fi but effectively impractical. Early models had many of the same limitations as the concept of time's first experiences with the mechanical clock: their range was modest, and while promising, their performance could not be compared to that of the traditional car. But just as the mechanical clock moved from novice to world-class professional, electric vehicles underwent rapid evolution.

With every technological advancement coming into play, the once-humble electric car found its confidence and voice.

The development of lithium-ion batteries became like discovering a strong and powerful new ally that saw a dramatic improvement in range and performance.

Before long, these vehicles turned from a niche market to a viable and desirable choice for consumers.

It was not a transition without its challenges. Many consumers, much like mechanical clock skeptics, were in disbelief about the feasibility of this new mode of transportation. Government incentives and subsidies served as guiding mentors, helping make the path wider for adoption.

Major automotive manufacturers, once quite skeptical, began to invest heavily in electric technology to join with fist raised in the air, the EV revolution.

By the mid-1910s, electric cars had done the work: no longer mere novelties to many but serious competition in the car world, market trends reflected this shift with electric vehicle sales climbing steadily (Archsmith, Muehlegger, & Rapson, 2021)[2].

What was once revolutionary became everyday life, much like the mystical magic of the mechanical clock's acceptance of its role in the modernizing world.

Studies and research began to unwrap the far-reaching effect of electric vehicles on our economy and environment. The mystical magic of the mechanical clock's battles against the hour glass, too, were in so many ways symbolic of how the rise of electric cars impinged upon everything from the way energy is produced to the very manufacturing of automobiles themselves. The journey of electric cars, from experimental prototypes to mainstream successes, stands testimony to the power of entrepreneurship and innovation in changing the world.

And so, the story of electric cars goes on - indeed promising to grow its effect over the human population in coming years.

Just as the mystical magic of the mechanical clock's adventures shaped its future, so the rise of electric vehicles is going to reshape our automotive landscape and change the corresponding economics.

This article reviews the early history of electric vehicles, including the contributions of visionaries like Ferdinand Porsche and Thomas Edison [1].

1: U.S. Department of Energy. (2014). History of the electric car. Retrieved October 12, 2024, from https://www.energy.gov/articles/history-electric-car

This paper discusses the adoption of electric vehicles in the United States, highlighting how by 2017, electric vehicles had gained significant acceptance as an alternative to gas-powered cars[2].

2: Archsmith, J. E., Muehlegger, E., & Rapson, D. S. (2021). Future paths of electric vehicle adoption in the United States: Predictable determinants, obstacles, and opportunities. National Bureau of Economic Research Working Paper No. 28933. National Bureau of Economic Research. https://doi.org/10.3386/w28933

CHAPTER 2:

ECONOMIC PRINCIPLES AND INFLATION

We'll use a little allegory for a while - In the flourishing town of Economicsville, where each marketplace and street vendor reverberated with the jingle of the coin against coin, the cha-ching of every transaction, there lived an old gray sage named Professor Read.

Professor Read was known for his deep understanding of how the world of money worked: there was a dance of numbers and theories behind every price tag and every budget. He loved nothing more than to lecture on inflation, a force as enigmatic as it is strong.

Professor Read could always be counted on to relate to his students the unfolding of the story of inflation. He'd begin with a simple story about a village that was not very different from Economicsville, except that in it, people produced and bartered for goods.

They lived in a world where the value of their currency could rise, or fall based on a variety of factors. In it, one coin bought a loaf of bread. Life was uncomplicated, and the villagers were happy.

One day, a mysterious traveler arrived in town, possessing a mysterious golden coin. This was the fabled golden coin that could multiply into more golden coins of its kind. The traveler convinced the ruler at the time to mandate that all market transactions be conducted with this magical coin.

The villagers were overjoyed when this traveler began raining the golden coins upon them.

They bought more bread, more clothes, and more trinkets. The market was flourishing, or so it seemed. But soon the golden coins started to have an unexpected impact.

As more and more coins came into circulation, the value of each one began to decrease.

Whereas villagers were once able to buy a loaf of bread for one coin, they soon found themselves having to use two, then three, then four for the very same purchase.

The golden coins had expanded or inflated the cost of goods in the market as a byproduct of the coin's ability to magically multiply itself, and the villagers realized their new lot in life wasn't quite as advantageous as they had once thought it to be.

Professor Read would lean in and explain that this was a tale about the cause of inflation. Inflation is merely the general increase in the price level of goods and services in a country (Congressional Research Service, 2023)[1].

This reduces the purchasing power of money. Too much money floating in an economy could raise prices for goods and services, just as those golden coins had done.

To further explain this, Professor Read compared inflation to a balloon: when you blow air into the balloon, it expands. Likewise, when there's an increase or you inflate the money supply, it can cause prices to expand.

This ballooning effect may be furthered by an increased demand for goods, higher production costs, or changes in monetary policy.

In Economicsville, inflation wasn't an abstract notion but very much a reality. Professor Read's students learned that all sectors contribute to inflation in one way or another. For example, if the village bakery has to pay more for wheat, then it will have to increase the price of its bread, which will in-turn cause the local deli to have to increase its price of delicious sandwiches. Likewise, if the price of oil increases, transportation may become more expensive, hence increasing the prices of many goods.

For instance, technological changes to methods of production lowers costs and helps to maintain lower prices, while disruptions in production or shortages can do the opposite.

How Different Sectors Contribute to Inflation

Inflation from the grand theater of economics sometimes plays the role of the protagonist, and other times it plays the role of the antagonist.

And just as each actor affects the plot in a different manner; each sector contributes something impactful to the story of inflation. Think of inflation as an ever-changing theatrical performance about rising prices, where every sector is a distinctly different actor or actress, playing their distinct role to contribute toward the staging.

The Stage is Set: What is Inflation?

Setting the stage before sector-specific performances, at its most basic and generic explanation, inflation is defined as a general increase in the price level of common goods and services over time (Congressional Research Service, 2023)[2].

That is why a dollar can buy less today compared to yesterday.

It may result from a number of variables that range from demand-pull inflation, cost-push inflation, to even built-in inflation (Schwarzer, 2018)[3].

The underlying equivalent of an economic drama, where inflation is a jolly riddler trickster, making too much demand chase after too few goods at one time and is lust driven by the rising costs of production.

But each sector added to this generally inflationary story bringing a new layer of nuance.

Let's start with one of the most powerful drivers of inflation:

The Energy Sector

Think of the energy sector as a powerhouse, driving not only our cars but also our economies (Kilian & Zhou, 2022)[4].

When the price of oil goes up, that is like putting it in the spotlight at center stage.

Increased energy costs tend to translate to higher prices for transportation, heating, and electricity, which in turn, tend to elevate the overall price for goods and services.

Think of it like owing the geopolitical tensions or disruptions in supply chains to a rise in the price of oil.

As gasoline becomes more costly, delivery costs for goods shoot up.

This increase in transportation expenses is passed down to consumers, making everything from groceries to gadgets costlier.

Hence, the energy sector's performance is strongly associated with inflationary trends.

Housing Market

Building up costs, we now turn to the housing market, where another act of our inflation drama is played.

Think of the housing market as the stage on which the underlying economy plays its role. When housing prices rise, for instance, it is not only about housing sales; the increase trickles onto to rental houses and apartments, cost of construction, and even to materials such as lumber and steel. Consider a tight housing market where demand is greater than supply.

Builders must pay more for land and more for materials, and such business costs are always passed on to the consuming homebuyers and renters.

Plus, increasing prices for homes can invoke the wealth effect: it would make homeowners feel richer, and they would spend more, adding to the inflationary pressures.

In this staging, the housing sector contributes to inflation through both direct and indirect channels.

Another vital thespian, the labor market adds its acting skills to this drama about inflation. Consider this sector to be the ensemble cast in which wage dynamics interact with the performance of the general economy.

In situations of low unemployment, jobs are widely available, and workers can bargain for higher wages.

Higher wages, though effective for employees, have the consequence of increasing production costs for employers.

Consider an example: a factory whose wages start to rise, increasing these costs could eventually be passed on to consumers in higher prices for goods.

It's a classic case of the cost-push inflation variety where increased production costs rise and, in turn, raise the consumer price level.

As we continue our travels through Economicsville, let's not forget the food sector, a segment where the inflationary pressures are both felt and are very real.

Food industries are the symphonic band located in the orchestra pit in our economic dramatic play, through which price changes are felt daily. The big factor that contributes to these changes is weather conditions, crop yields, and supply chain disruptions.

For instance, a drought and subsequently poor crop yields can make fresh produce prices skyrocket. The increased prices of food strains budgets at home and add to inflation.

It is also a very direct compliment to inflation, often highly visible, as consumers feel the pain right at the checkout counter.

The Tech Sector: Innovation and Inflation

We finally turn to the technology sector which, although commonly linked to price deflation because of its rapid pace of innovation, also has a role to play in inflation.

Technology can be thought of as a two-edged sword: on one hand, innovations may lead to more efficient production and therefore, to lower costs (Lv, Liu, & Xu, 2019)[5]; on the other hand, rapid changes in technology result in higher costs for products and services that represent the latest word in science. For instance, some of these new technologies or gadgets come with premium prices.

In many instances, when tech companies invest in research and development, these costs are reflected in the price tags of the new products.

Besides, as technology becomes integral to life, a disruption in supply creation or shortage of components tends to have a spiraling effect on inflation. This was evident with Japan's 2011 earthquake and tsunami the caused a rocket price increase in RAM memory chips as markets displayed concern over fabrication plant shutdowns, power outages and supply chain shortages (U.S. Bureau of Labor Statistics, 2011)[6].

Every sector is adding its own acting skills to the inflationary theatrical production, whether it be increasing energy costs, bustling housing markets, wage dynamics, an upward sloping shift from left to right of food prices, or technology in constant flux.

The Role of Technological Advancements in Economic Shifts

Knowing how all these different sectors connect and influence inflation in general helps us better understand the complexity of the economic stage.

It will be important, therefore, to appreciate how the performance of each sector ripples through the economy to shape the broader inflationary trends we experience in our journey through the electric vehicle revolution and its impact on inflation.

Technological advancement acts like the architects of change within the large and changing building structure that is our economy.

They build new structures, reshape existing ones, and sometimes even tear down the old to make way for the new.

To understand how technology drives economic shifts and influences inflation, let's once again use allegory to journey through this dynamic interplay. Imagine if you will it's the late 18th century, and we're standing in a bustling textile factory in England.

The loud clatter of looms is everywhere; workers are running about, accomplishing their mission with the newest technological marvels of their time: the spinning jenny and the power loom (Allen, 2018) [6].

This invention started revolutionizing the textile industry by allowing mass production of goods at a much lower cost compared with fabrics.

As such new machines start coming into factories, they break an existing economic balance. What once took a lot of time and effort suddenly becomes highly efficient.

Textiles become cheaper, and the struggle for clothes among the common masses is solved.

This scene epitomizes how technological progress fosters prices and creates economic change: an early example of how innovation can lead to dramatic changes in inflation dynamics.

Fast forward to the late 20th century, and we find ourselves standing in the middle of a bustling Silicon Valley office surrounded by early computer scientists and engineers.

The hum of computers and the clacking of keyboards echo through this room, filled with excitement about a new, revolutionizing innovation: the at-home personal computer.

Work and home environments will never be the same again upon the introduction of personal computers.

Businesses are better equipped to streamline operations now, and personal access to information and communication tools increases on an unprecedented level.

This technological leap can therefore have a strong effect on productivity surges and, by consequence, on economic shifts. With personal computers becoming more accessible to the population, the computers also become cheaper.

The falling prices of the technology products reflect increases in production efficiency and competition among firms in the tech industry. This scenario illustrates how technological progress can reduce costs to the consumer and influence inflation by pushing down the prices of goods and services, while it enhances economic productivity.

Let's enter a modern manufacturing plant where the new workers are robots and automated systems.

Now, imagine the scene where humans are standing, guiding rows of robotic arms assembling products with precision and speed.

It looks like a symphony of mechanical efficiency on the production floor, as automation pushes production to new dimensions.

Automation is quite a giant technological shift where, instead of depending on human labor, businesses can fall back on machinery for higher volumes of production with reduced costs.

This scene showcases the dual impact of automation: while it can lead to lower prices for manufactured goods due to reduced production costs, it also has implications for unemployment rates and wages.

Workers who once did manual tasks are now required to adapt to new roles or face job displacement.

It could affect inflation in two ways: first, through better efficiency, thus lower prices of goods; second, through compensation adjustments and employment patterns.

Coming back to the present world, "green technology" has become a topic of great interest. Imagine yourself standing at a solar farm, with rows of shiny, mirrored solar panels that harness and transform sunlight into usable energy in your home or factory.

Now not too far down the road from you, in a different locale, the turbines of a wind farm rotate smoothly with the breeze and sends wind generated energy into a food storage warehouse.

The rise of green technology signifies a significant shift in our energy sourcing and usage. Solar and wind power are becoming more mainstream, leading to a reduction in our reliance on fossil fuels.

This technological advance presents an opportunity and a challenge at the same time.

Higher initial investment in green technology increases costs temporarily, while in the longer term, better efficiency and reduced dependence on non-renewable resources drive energy prices down (Wang, Li, & Liao, 2021)[7].

This latter scenario demonstrates how technological changes in energy production can impact inflation through changes in the cost structure of energy and overall economic dynamics.

This report defines inflation as a general increase in the price level of goods and services in a country[1&2].
1 & 2: Congressional Research Service. (2023). Introduction to U.S. Economy: Inflation. CRS Report No. IF10477. Congressional Research Service. https://crsreports.congress.gov/product/pdf/IF/IF10477

This paper addresses the conflicting views on inflation[3].
3: Schwarzer, J. A. (2018). Retrospectives: Cost-Push and Demand-Pull Inflation: Milton Friedman and the "Cruel Dilemma." Journal of Economic Perspectives, 32(1), 195-210. https://doi.org/10.1257/jep.32.1.195

This paper discusses how energy price shocks contribute to inflation, highlighting the significant role of the energy sector[4].
4: Kilian, L., & Zhou, X. (2022). A broader perspective on the inflationary effects of energy price shocks. Federal Reserve Bank of Dallas Working Paper No. 2224. https://doi.org/10.24149/wp2224

This paper discusses how technological progress and globalization have played a significant role in influencing inflation[5].
5: Lv, L., Liu, Z., & Xu, Y. (2019). Technological progress, globalization and low-inflation: Evidence from the United States. PLOS ONE, 14(4), e0215366. https://doi.org/10.1371/journal.pone.0215366

This report examines how the earthquake and tsunami affected import prices, including RAM prices, due to supply chain disruptions and production halts in Japan[6].
6: U.S. Bureau of Labor Statistics. (2011). Import and Export Prices: Third Quarter 2011. U.S. Bureau of Labor Statistics. https://www.bls.gov/opub/btn/archive/the-impact-of-the-earthquake-in-japan-on-us-imports.pdf

This article discusses how the invention of the power loom impacted 18th century England, particularly focusing on the economic and social changes it brought about[7].

7: Allen, R. C. (2018). The hand-loom weaver and the power loom: A Schumpeterian perspective. European Review of Economic History, 22(4), 381-402.

https://doi.org/10.1093/ereh/hex030

This paper reviews recent studies on the short and long-term effects of converting to renewable energy sources on the U.S. economy, discussing both the initial costs and the long-term benefits[8].

8: Wang, M., Li, Y., & Liao, G. (2021). Research on the impact of green technology innovation on energy total factor productivity, based on provincial data of China. Frontiers in Environmental Science, 9, 710931.

https://doi.org/10.3389/fenvs.2021.710931

CHAPTER 3:

CASE STUDIES

At the heart of our story, in the place where the rise of electric cars meets the world of economics, we take a journey through several lands affected by this automotive revolution.

Each of these diverse lands carries a very special allegorical tale of insight into how the rising star, which is the electric car, has influenced inflation and economic dynamics.

The Tale of Green Valley

Our starting point is the attractive Green Valley situated amidst the hills. The village of Green Valley has always been popular for its ever-appealing, green-sprawling scenery and a very close-knit community.

Recently, Hunter, the mayor of this town, took up the initiative to change the entire fleet of municipal vehicles into electric ones.

Hunter had a dream of having a clean environment and to decrease dependence on fossil fuel.

The people of Green Valley were thrilled at first. They welcomed the shiny new electric buses and maintenance vehicles into their community with open arms.

But over time, an unexpected turn of events began to take hold. The town's demand for electricity began spiking exponentially while the local power plant was not in a position to respond to the boom. The increased demand for electricity means increased utility bills for residents and a higher cost of living in the area.

Economists visiting Green Valley also noticed that although the shift to electric vehicles did reduce emissions, it was also one of the contributing factors to inflationary pressures within the town.

The story of Green Valley showed that moving to electric vehicles had a ripple, affecting not just the environment but the economic balance of the community.

The Story of Silicon Bluff

Now we travel to the bustling tech hub of Silicon Bluff, known for its innovative spirit. Silicon Bluff was among those very first cities to adopt electric cars, and had several technology companies that actually led the way towards an EV revolution.

Soon, their roads were filled with sleeker and sleeker electric cars, each one more advanced than the last. This rapid move into electric vehicles brought problems of their own.

The demand for high-tech components like batteries and microchips increased, leading to shortages and price increases in these vital materials (Argonne National Laboratory, 2021)[1].

This, in turn, drove up the production costs of electric cars and, subsequently, their retail prices.

Silicon Bluff's story is a manifestation of how rapid growth in electric vehicle adoption creates bottlenecks in the supply chain, leading to upward price pressures.

The high demand for specialized parts not only increased car prices but also had far-reaching consequences through the economy, pushing up the cost of technology and innovation throughout the city.

The Chronicles of Emerald Ridge

Our last allegorical destination will be to Emerald Ridge, which is considered one of the most concerned places about environmental sustainability.

Thus, Emerald Ridge had welcomed electric cars with open arms: hefty investment in infrastructure, such as charging stations and subsidies for electric car buyers.

At an initial stage, everything went smoothly in Emerald Ridge. The transition was easy, but then the very attractive incentives offered by the government resulted in a huge surge in electric car purchases.

While this growth in sales was indicative of the land's interest in green technology, there was also an ulterior effect of this growth.

An increase in electronic vehicle owners increased demand for rare earth metals used in the batteries, driving prices up on the global market (Fishman, Myers, Rios, & Graedel, 2018)[2]. This is an example of how government policy on electric vehicles can have a very deep, relative economic impact.

One of the contributors to inflation was the increase in the prices of materials, a fact in which showed that incentives, while driving positive changes in the environment, do have their problems on the economic front that must be carefully managed.

With the stories of Green Valley, Silicon Bluff, and Emerald Ridge, as the reader, you will be able to achieve a better understanding regarding the economic outcomes of this electric car revolution.

Each of these stories unfolds one part of how this technological shift is impinging upon inflation and economic dynamics. From local challenges in Green Valley, to the chain of supply in Silicon Bluff, to material costs in Emerald Ridge, these case studies drive home the need for balance between technological progress and economic stability in various ways.

Technological Change and Economic Transformation

In the theater of economic transformation, technological changes are the real after-party of our theatrical play about electric vehicles and inflation.

They don't just change the script, they rewrite it. We shall utilize more research to delve into the case studies of how technological innovations have altered not only industries but also shifted the economic paradigms sometimes with dramatic consequences.

Scenario: In the late 1990s, the whole world was going gaga over a new technological wonder, the Internet. Now imagine a walk-through Silicon Valley at this time, with its tech entrepreneurs and venture capitalists riding high on the promise of the 'dot com boom'. The rise of the Internet was more than just a technological phenomenon but a seismic shift that reached into almost every nook and cranny of the economy.

Amazon and eBay appeared out of this digital ether with the promise of changing the way people would shop and trade. Through mass hype and speculation, technology firms saw their stock prices soar high as the investor world watched in awe.

This was the phase in which heavy investments were placed in technology infrastructure. This plunged Internet related jobs and completely changed the face of consumer behavior (Charlesworth, 2024)[3].

E-commerce became a household name as traditional retail houses needed to continue striving just to survive. High inflationary tendencies plagued the boom in the tech stocks as eager investors put in their money in newer and newer ventures.

But the year 2000 saw the burst of the 'dot com' bubble, and with it came the realization that technological revolutions can give way to some dizzying highs, as well as steep declines (Schubert, Gavurová, Kováč, & Užík, 2015)[4].

This case study epitomizes how technological advances might bring in fast paced economic changes, creating new markets and opportunities, but at the same time bringing risks and uncertainties.

Now, let's come back to the early 2000s and zero in on another game changer, the smartphone. Take, for instance, in 1999, the first commercial camera phone, called the Kyocera Visual Phone VP-210, while this phone predates the early 2000s by a few months, it's still close enough to include in our timeline. Then in 2002 BlackBerry released the BlackBerry 5810 the company's first smartphone. In 2007 the launching event of the first iPhone, signified a definite communication revolution whereby cell phone companies began to introduce technologies that was to change the face of communication, business, and bring about never thought about lifestyle changes (Sela, Rozenboim, & Ben-Gal, 2022)[5]. The rise of the smartphone was nothing less than revolutionary, it captured in one pocket sized device computing power, connectivity, and entertainment.

It moved a whole new ecosystem of uses, from social media to mobile banking, and utterly shifted how people interact and spend.

Economically, the smartphone revolution ignited a whole new era of consumer spending and investment.

From the corporations engaged in telecommunications to those developing software, all prospered. Mobile commerce brought in new inflationary dynamics; super profits for the technology companies, while old businesses struggled with the paradigm shift (Statista, 2024)[6].

But most importantly, the impact of the smartphone was across consumer markets. It altered the fate of travel, entertainment, even health industries.

For instance, in many locations, telemedicine became more available, expanding the health services' reach but simultaneously placing new economic pressures on traditional health care models (Pearl & Wayling, 2022)[7].

Now, let's come to the green technology revolution. Just imagine standing on an extended farm with solar installations or a wind turbine installation at the latest stage.

These various symbols of environmental progress have also made the current economic shift in the direction of sustainable energy.

Certain technological developments with regards to solar panels, wind turbines, and means of energy storage have led to the rise of green technology.

This had the final consequence of drastically lowering the price of renewable energy and thus made entire traditional fossil fuel industries obsolete while reshaping global energy markets.

For instance, countries such as Germany and Denmark have been leading the way in the use of green technology by investing billions of pounds into renewable energy sources (McKinsey & Company, 2023)[8].

These have led to significant reductions in carbon emissions and energy costs. However, economic shifts persist as traditional energy sectors decline and new ones emerge, driving job creation and economic growth within the green tech sector.

Yet, this shift has not been without its own casualties.

High initial costs of the infrastructure for green technology, and to an extent, the role of policy mechanisms in propelling the technology at play, have contributed to economic snags.

This case study shall further help illustrate how shifts in energy technology can create upward yet complex economic shifts.

The Rise of Artificial Intelligence and Automation

Let's consider the newest frontier: that of artificial intelligence - AI and automation.

Imagine being taken through a modern warehouse where even the inventories and fulfillment of orders were done so precisely by robots and AI systems. AI and automation are breaking grounds in industries ranging from manufacturing to finance.

For instance, AI driven algorithms optimize supply chains, automate customer service, and enhance data analytics (McKinsey & Company, 2022)[9].

The economic impacts brought about by AI and automation are extremely impactful. The same forces that propel productivity, reducing costs for businesses, which may or may not be passed on to consumers, also bring in issues related to job displacement and the need to acquire new skills.

The AI and automation shift, while they provide incredible opportunities for growth and efficiency brought about by technological changes, this also means adaptation and strategic planning to dampen the unintended economic effects.

New challenges and opportunities set in place by these advancements reshape consumer behavior, industry practice, and economic dynamics.

These case studies help deepen you as the reader's evaluation of the complex role that technology can play in driving the underlying economic shifts in inflationary trends.

The shift into electric cars has consequences that are multilayered and economic by nature, and shall be demonstrated by analyzing these stories.

These case studies will illuminate the trajectory towards a future characterized by electric vehicles, underscoring their profound implications for the global economy.

The study discusses the challenges in the supply chain for lithium-ion batteries, which are critical for electric vehicles[1].
1: Argonne National Laboratory. (2021). A 10-year look at the battery supply chain in America. U.S. Department of Energy. https://www.anl.gov/article/a-10year-look-at-the-battery-supply-chain-in-america

This study examines how the increasing adoption of electric vehicles in the United States is driving up the demand and prices for rare earth metals used in their batteries[2].
2: Fishman, T., Myers, R. J., Rios, O., & Graedel, T. E. (2018). Implications of emerging vehicle technologies on rare earth supply and demand in the United States. Resources, 7(1), 9. https://doi.org/10.3390/resources7010009

This article discusses the rise and fall of internet startups during the dot-com bubble, emphasizing the valuable lessons learned from this period of market volatility[3].
3: Charlesworth, J. (2024). The Dot-Com Bubble: Lessons from the Boom and Bust of Internet Startups. Haystack Blog. https://www.haystackapp.io/resources/the-dot-com-bubble-lessons-from-the-boom-and-bust-of-internet-startups

This study analyzes various market indicators to compare their performance during the Dot-Com Bubble[4].
4: Schubert, W., Gavurová, B., Kováč, V., & Užík, M. (2015). Comparison of Selected Market Indicators During the Dot-Com Bubble. In S. Gokten & G. Kucukkocaoglu (Eds.), Financial Management from an Emerging Market Perspective (pp. 123-145). IntechOpen. https://doi.org/10.5772/intechopen.71381

This study investigates how smartphone use impacts the quality of life for both older and younger adults in the United States, highlighting significant changes in their daily lives[5].
5: Sela, A., Rozenboim, N., & Ben-Gal, H. C. (2022). Smartphone use behavior and quality of life: What is the role of awareness?. PloS one, 17(3), e0260637. https://doi.org/10.1371/journal.pone.0260637

The Statista page on online shopping highlights the significant growth of mobile commerce, driven by consumer preferences for convenience, advancements in technology, and retailers' adaptations to enhance the mobile shopping experience[6].
6: Statista. (2024). Online shopping - statistics & facts. Retrieved October 12, 2024, from https://www.statista.com/topics/871/online-shopping/#topicOverview

This article discusses how the rise of telehealth has expanded healthcare access while also introducing new economic pressures on traditional healthcare systems[7].

7: Pearl, R., & Wayling, B. (2022, May 10). The telehealth era is just beginning. Harvard Business Review. https://hbr.org/2022/05/the-telehealth-era-is-just-beginning

This article discusses the potential for U. S. green banks to deliver significant environmental and economic impacts through strategic financing of sustainable projects[8].

8: McKinsey & Company. (2023, April 20). Delivering impact from US green bank financing. McKinsey & Company Insights. https://www.mckinsey.com/capabilities/sustainability/our-insights/delivering-impact-from-us-green-bank-financing

The article discusses how consumer goods companies leverage autonomous supply chain planning to enhance efficiency, responsiveness, and decision-making through advanced technologies and data analytics[9].

9: McKinsey & Company. (2022, March 2). Better supply-chain planning with AI and machine learning. McKinsey Insights. https://www.mckinsey.com/capabilities/operations/our-insights/autonomous-supply-chain-planning-for-consumer-goods-companies

CHAPTER 4:

THE PSYCHOLOGICAL AND SOCIAL IMPACT

Next in our saga of the electric car revolution, we will set our sights on the less obvious but equally fascinating effects that electric cars have on human behavior and social dynamics.

Envision a world where EVs will change not only the way people travel but even the very core of the human way of thinking and interaction.

In this chapter, we will give an overview of the whimsical yet profound changes electric cars bring into our lives, both psychologically and socially.

The Chronicles of Green Acres

Let us embark on a journey in Green Acres, the place to be, where one would feel like eco-friendly living is definitely for me. Nestled amongst sprawling hills and vibrant fields spreading out so far and wide, a perfect place for people who want to escape the big city life, and just want that countryside (Mizzy, 1965)[1].

Green Acres was a town known for its close-knit community and beautiful landscape. The promise of electric cars heralded a new chapter in this much-loved storybook; silent EVs made their first entries into this charming hamlet. The residents were full of anticipation and hope. Mayor Olive was a champion of sustainability, and under her leadership, in came electric buses, in came community charging stations.

At first, the residents were thrilled! The streets grew quieter, the air cleansed itself, and Green Acres seemed to shine with rejuvenated energy. But beneath the surface of this apparent utopia, unexpected psychological shifts began to take place within the town.

In fact, it turned out that the silence of electric cars was serene and gave rise to a few curious incidents, 'phantom vehicle syndrome' (BMJ Group, 2023)[2].

Townspeople were accustomed to the rumble of the traditional engines, near-silent EVs put them into shock.

Children in the park, their shrieks of surprise were almost predictable upon the sudden appearance of a car seemingly out of nowhere. The customers at the local diner would jest that they were learning to appreciate the art of 'hearing' cars not by their roars, but by their subtle whooshes.

Meanwhile, Basil the former mechanic and now EV consultant became something of a local celebrity.

His makeover from 'Basil the Mechanic' to 'Basil the EV Whisperer' was a hit. His writings "Charge of Confidence: Conquering Range Anxiety with Your Electric Vehicle", on EV maintenance and alleviating worry about the distance owners can travel on a single charge, were sought after as fervently as the town's apple pie recipes. Basil's workshops, "Charging Your EV without Losing Your Sanity", which both are actually available from the large online book retailer, were always standing-room-only events. The transition had transformed not only the town's infrastructure but launched a cultural renaissance for all things electric vehicle.

The Saga of Techville

The next stop takes us to the core of the sprawling metropolis of Techville, where innovation and competition walk together hand in hand. Techville was no stranger to leading-edge tech, and the introduction of electric cars saw enthusiastic interest bordering on obsession. The neon lights that sparked in the city's skyline were now joined by the dazzling ads of the latest electric vehicle models.

Electric cars received face value when it came to being the coolest status symbol to acquire in Techville. Owning the most recent, gaudiest model was a matter of pride, and the city's social scene mirrored this preoccupation (Pew Research Center, 2023)[3]. The trend led to some hilarious and competitive behaviors.

At social gatherings, it's not unusual to hear people discussing the latest EV features and debating the merits of different battery technologies. One person might even tease another for having a 2025 model when they themselves have the newer, more advanced 2026 edition.

This had its psychological impact. The comparisons created something now widely known as 'EV FOMO' Fear of Missing Out (MacInnis & Krosnick, 2020)[4].

Those residents who couldn't keep up with the latest model would often find themselves in a mental slump, somehow thinking that their social worth was connected with the horsepower of their electric car.

What started out as an ecologically conscious decision soon turned into a source of anxiety for many when the burden of trying to be abreast of the most recent EV fashions became, to a great degree, an almost competitive sport.

They responded to this new dynamic by organizing an annual event called 'Techville EV Expo', a showy event of the latest and greatest in electric vehicles, half car show, half social spectacle.

The expo was an opportunity for extravagance from interactive holographic dashboards to autonomous driving capabilities. Its unofficial motto: "Keeping up with the Joneses, but in a zero-emission way!".

The Fable of Eco Valley

Our last stop will be the community in Eco Valley serene and idyllic, where green living is more than a trend, it is a coveted way of life.

The people of the valley embraced electric cars with open arms, impelled by their commitment to reducing their carbon footprint. It was a transition celebrated smoothly with activities on conservation from the community and educational workshops on sustainability.

The social impact was heavy here in Eco Valley. It drew this rather small community together even further through their shared vision of environmental good stewardship.

Yet, at the same time, that very focus on green technology gave way to some interesting dynamics for displays of grandstanding, socially speaking. What used to be a simple potluck dinner, the annual 'Eco Gala', had now evolved into a competition of eco-friendly innovations where residents tried to outcompete each other with the most creative solution to green problems.

It included the 'Silent Car Race', where people race their electric vehicles in complete silence.

Although the race is less about speed and more about ingenuity, it became a highlight of the year. Whimsical features adorned residents' cars, like solar powered disco lights and animated dashboards that played catchy environmental slogans.

Thus, this great event was one full of competition and camaraderie combined, reflecting the community's commitment to fun and sustainability (Barrón, Gruber, & Huffman, 2022)[5].

This at times led to humorous debates, such as the hotly contested debate over what shade of green was superior for an electric car: Emerald Envy or Forest Fantasy? Despite the light-heartedness of such discussions, they underlined the societal importance that was placed on green living in Eco Valley.

Revealing the Impact

A suburban neighborhood in the early 2010s. The hum of electric cars brings the streets to life, and it seems there is an air of excitement among its residents. In one of its driveways, a professional couple proudly display their new electric vehicle, a sleek model boasting environmental benefits with the latest in technological advancement.

The scene caught the fervor of the early adopters, that first wave of consumers who wanted to be at the forefront of new technologies. They are one of the first wave of EV adopters; people who often exclaim to be more environmentally concerned and fascinated with trying out new technology. Similarly, such people are generally very satisfied with their choice, look forward to their next EV purchase, and may even experience positive psychological effects (J.D. Power, 2021)[7].

The self-labeled environmentalists that owned EVs before 2020, some even purchasing way back in 2010 - early adopters raise their self-esteem and social status through the eco-friendly choices they make. The psychological boost comes from aligning their actions with values, contributing to a positive self-image and the feeling of belonging to a progressive movement.

From working our way through the narratives of Green Acres, Techville, and Eco Valley, it becomes clear that the rising prominence of electric vehicles represents far more than a seemingly earth-friendly technological phenomenon. The story of electric car adoption reshapes psychological landscapes and social engagements of the most captivating textured canvas of impasto.

From the charming vagaries of phantom vehicles in Green Acres to the competitive EV culture of Techville and to the communalist spirit of Eco Valley, these vignettes indicate something of the rich impact of electric cars on human action.

Through the psychological effects of social influence within the whirlwind of technological and economic changes that come along with the electric vehicle, there is much more at play than market fluctuations and environmental benefits.

There is a silo of psychological and social impacts beneath the surface when it comes to the economic, functional, and social factors influencing electric vehicles ownership (Xia, Wu, & Zhang, 2022)[6].

It Started, and it Picked Up Pace Quickly.

Imagine a city so teeming that electric cars would no longer raise eyebrows with regards to commonness. Well, not everyone is exactly on board with the shift.

A middle-aged professional sits in a busy city café, sipping his coffee as he talks with his friend about how expensive electric vehicles are. "I want to go green," he says, "but the cost is a huge barrier." This unease or tension that this scene points to is an example of cognitive dissonance many consumers feel (Davis, 2023)[8]. While the awareness of the benefits of electric vehicles is increasing, the psychological strain of how to balance personal finance and environmental values is palpable.

Many consumers must suffer through some sort of psychological discomfort whenever their environmental values conflict with financial constraints. This cognitive dissonance thus gives way to frustration and guilt, reflecting in overall satisfaction and adoption rates.

Social Dynamics in Electric Vehicle Adoption

Imagine going to that community meeting where the recent evolving of electric vehicles is the hot debate of the day.

With positive discussions filling the room in showing off their EVs proudly while others seemed skeptical, we ponder the social influence of electric vehicle adoption. The attendees scrutinize the opportunity cost through the lens of pre-existing schema, social norms, and peer influence, thereby shaping their attitudes towards the assimilation of novel data and emerging technologies.

When people see others around them driving electric vehicles, they are much more likely to be encouraged and make a purchase themselves. The social influence is both positive and negative, it enhances the adoption rate of EVs through peer pressure, while negative social responses, or perceived ridicule, will scare people off from making the switch. This social dynamic highlights how individual decision-making influences and is influenced by larger societal trends.

Much like the modern day Griswold's planning a family trip to the mega-theme park, technology enthusiasts who would otherwise purchase EVs without hesitation, still evaluate family road trips in all electric EVs with a tinge of anxiety (Hughes, 1983)[9]. Laying out a route, frustration and relief intermingle as they study the charging station locations and type. The absence of widespread charging and quick-charging infrastructure has started to turn psychological, affecting travel plans and overall travel experiences.

There is a psychological effect on electric vehicle owners when considering the current charging infrastructure. EV travelers' perceived anxiety and overall satisfaction are crucially influenced by the availability and accessibility of charging stations (Halbey, Kowalewski, & Ziefle, 2015)[10].

While these issues are indeed being addressed by improvement in charging technology, in the transition phase, psychological stress is experienced.

The feeling of uncertainty and strategic planning dampens the enthusiasm of even the most dedicated owners of EVs.

Now, let's move forward into a future where electric vehicles have been further immersed in daily life.

Imagine a world where EVs are just as common as traditional cars, and the technology has blended into everyday life. Years down the line, how do people feel about this transition?

Over time, consumers are generally satisfied and have a deeper sense of accomplishment regarding their choice (Hoang, Pham, & Vu, 2022)[11].

When electric cars finally reach a threshold of familiarity that its predecessor had to do during the days of horse-drawn carriages, this will give the green light for getting over anxiety regarding ownership. As previously noted, long-term owners demonstrate a significant congruence between their personal values and daily decisions, thereby fostering enduring positive psychological impacts and an enhanced sense of environmental stewardship (AAA Newsroom, 2020)[12].

As we conclude this chapter, it is evident that the psychological and social effects of electric vehicles are just as multi-layered and multi-dimensional as the technology itself.

From initial excitement over early adopters, through the difficult phase of mainstream adoption to the long-term psychological benefits, the human factor is right at the center of the story of technological progress.

The psychological effects take us one more step into understanding the holistic impacts of electric vehicles in society. It is a reminder that behind every technological shift lies a very human story, one filled with aspirations, challenges, and evolving perceptions.

The psychological and social effects of electric vehicles are as diverse and dynamic as the cars themselves.

So, they have revealed how technological advancement, while transformative, also weaves new threads into the fabric of our social lives.

In the end, the journey of electric vehicles is not just a story of technological progress, but also of human adaptation, humor, and community spirit.

Vic Mizzy composed the memorable theme song for the television show Green Acres in 1965[1].

1: Mizzy, V. (1965). Green Acres theme song. In Green Acres (TV show). NBC Television.

This article highlights that pedestrians in urban areas may be twice as likely to be hit by electric and hybrid cars compared to traditional petrol or diesel ones[2].
2: BMJ Group. (2023, October 13). Pedestrians may be twice as likely to be hit by electric and hybrid cars as petrol or diesel ones. BMJ Group. https://bmjgroup.com/pedestrians-may-be-twice-as-likely-to-be-hit-by-electric-hybrid-cars-as-petrol-diesel-ones/

This article explores Americans' perceptions of electric vehicles, highlighting the reasons why some people are likely to consider an electric vehicle for their next purchase[3].
3: Pew Research Center. (2023, July 13). How Americans view electric vehicles. Pew Research Center.
https://www.pewresearch.org/short-reads/2023/07/13/how-americans-view-electric-vehicles/

This article provides insights into American perceptions and resistance toward electric vehicles, highlighting environmental psychology factors influencing ownership[4].
4: MacInnis, B., & Krosnick, J. A. (2020, October 19). Climate insights 2020: Electric vehicles. Resources for the Future.
https://www.rff.org/publications/reports/climateinsights2020-electric-vehicles/

This article highlights how ecocomposition classrooms and related events bring students together to actively engage in environmental awareness and climate change discussions[5].
5: Barrón, N. G., Gruber, S., & Huffman, G. (2022). Student engagement and environmental awareness: Gen Z and ecocomposition. Environmental Humanities, 14(1), 219-232. https://doi.org/10.1215/22011919-9481528

This is an article discussing the types of Americans who are likely to consider buying an EV and the reasons why[6].
6: Xia, Z., Wu, D., & Zhang, L. (2022). Economic, functional, and social factors influencing electric vehicles' adoption: An empirical study based on the diffusion of innovation theory. Sustainability, 14(10), 6283. https://doi.org/10.3390/su14106283

This study finds that most EV owners in the US are satisfied and likely to repurchase an EV[7].
7: J.D. Power. (2021, January). 2021 U.S. Electric Vehicle Experience (EVX) Ownership Study. https://www.jdpower.com/business/press-releases/2021-us-electric-vehicle-experience-evx-ownership-study

This is an article about the reasons why many Americans are not buying electric vehicles[8].
8: Davis, M. (2023, March 6). High costs and safety concerns: Why millions of Americans aren't buying electric vehicles. https://www.valuepenguin.com/electric-vehicle-concerns-survey

National Lampoon's Vacation is a 1983 comedy film about a family's chaotic road trip to Wally World, with Clark Griswold as the main character, played by Chevy Chase[9].
9: Hughes, J. (Writer). (1983). National Lampoon's Vacation [Motion picture]. Warner Bros. https://www.warnerbros.com/movies/national-lampoons-vacation

This reference explores user acceptance criteria for long-distance electric vehicle travel, framed as a fictional road trip experience[10].
10: Halbey, J., Kowalewski, S., & Ziefle, M. (2015). Going on a road-trip with my electric car: Acceptance criteria for long-distance use of electric vehicles. In A. Marcus (Ed.), experience, and usability: Interactive experience design. DUXU 2015. Lecture notes in computer science (Vol. 9188). Springer, Cham. https://doi.org/10.1007/978-3-319-20889-3_44

This study systematically reviews the factors influencing the transition from intention to actual behavior in adopting battery electric vehicles[11].
11: Hoang, T. T., Pham, H. T., & Vu, H. M. T. (2022). From intention to actual behavior to adopt battery electric vehicles: A systematic literature review. The Open Transportation Journal, 16(e2208100). https://doi.org/10.2174/18744478-v16-e2208100

This AAA report from 2020 explores the costs associated with electric vehicle ownership, along with consumer attitudes and behaviors towards EVs[12].

12: AAA Newsroom. (2020). Electric vehicle ownership: Cost, attitudes and behaviors. https://newsroom.aaa.com/wp-content/uploads/2020/11/True-Cost-of-EV-Ownership-and-EV-Owner-Sentiment-Fact-Sheet-Jan-2020.pdf

CHAPTER 5:

POLICY AND REGULATION

Electric cars are positioned within a broader context where technology intersects with daily life, with government policies and regulations forming a critical part of their operational environment. These policies shape and direct the trajectory of the electric vehicle revolution through strategic frameworks and legislative measures.

This chapter delves into how government policies have become the pivotal yet understated motivator of the electric car narrative, using allegory to make the reader more comfortable with the economic concepts being presented. By weaving in a touch of humor, we aim to keep the narrative engaging while exploring the intricacies of electric vehicle ownership.

Legal Enchanted Scrolls

Our story takes place in the busy capital of Politicstown, where the famously dressed and paper-carrying policymakers were just about to embark on a transformational judicial pursuit.

With the electric car arriving, a golden opportunity arose for these policymakers to draft new legislation and incentives aimed at boosting green futuristic orientations.

Politicstown was nothing less than a grand sight: hallowed marble halls of legislation, the weight of representation over drafting tables, pens in hand, twirling them around like mechanical magic wands.

Hot debates raged on over tax credits, rebates, and incentives that would make electric vehicles more palatable to the masses.

Among the most touted policies was the publicly branded *EV Incentive Act*, a law promising rich rebates to those who would buy electric vehicles. It was proposed as a financial pain reliever for buyers and making EVs not just an eco-friendly choice but one that was economically shrewd.

It meant everything, from tax breaks that offer discounts on home charging stations to various incentives to reduce barriers to entry for potential electric car owners (Javadnejad, Jahanbakh, Pinto, & Saeidi, 2023)[1].

It was not all rebates that one could get excited about. Politicstown then brought in the *Charging Infrastructure Expansion Act* that proposed pragmatic investments in charging stations. Picture in your mind a team of policy makers, Department of Transportation civil engineers, Department of Electricity zoning directors, and entrepreneurs, working night and day to create a pervasive web of charging points across the land so no electric car owner would ever have to face the countryside of 'low battery' despair (U.S. Department of Transportation, 2023)[2].

Economic Incentives: Mechanical clock

With the policies in their full swing of being framed, we return to the city of Eco Valley, which was to present the grand debut. The bustling city of Eco Valley had already been prominent for environmental awareness and welcomed these new incentives gladly.

Local government, eager to promote sustainability, enthusiastically championed electric vehicles, encouraging citizens to adopt this greener transportation option. As a result, many residents turned to the large online book retailer to purchase a comprehensive guide titled, 'Beyond the Battery: Your Journey and Guide to a Greener Commute', on transitioning to an electric vehicle, exploring topics such as trade-ins, leasing, financing, and calculating the break-even point compared to traditional gasoline cars.

Soon, electric vehicles would swell the streets of Eco Valley, and with that came a buzz in the air, a new opportunity. The masses loved the *EV Incentive Act* because now electric cars could be reasonably attained.

The local car dealerships advertising tax credits and rebates welcomed scores of eager customers (Rapson & Muehlegger, 2021)[3]. It was like the electric car became some sort of royal carriage, and everyone wanted in on this eco-friendly action.

But the fanfare also brought some humor. The local Eco-Fair, once a subdued market for organic fruits, vegetables, and crafts, had been invaded by electric cars.

Hawkers of all varieties of solar-powered doohickeys proliferated, including an 'ecofriendly car accessories' section at the farmers' market.

One entrepreneurial businessman hawked an '*I Love My EV*' bumper stickers, which appeared to adorn one-third of all cars in town overnight.

The Great Search for a Policy Equilibrium

No story has its glories without its thorns. The policymakers, yet again, had to strike the balance between incentives given and long-term sustainability when electric cars started gaining popularity. There was the formation of the 'Green Energy Task Force', a group that comprised policymaking stalwarts and environmentalists, to lead the charge in ensuring that the incentives offered did not bring along a different kind of boomerang.

One of the major quandaries was how to balance the introduction of EVs and the economic effect it would have on more traditional automotive sectors.

Political leaders wryly compared themselves to a circus juggler, keeping several flaming torches, or economic sectors, in the air without dropping any. The task force worked to devise policies that favored the transition to electric cars and provided them with support in terms of manpower and industries related to this transition (The Climate Group, 2021)[4].

The solution came in the form of a comprehensive 'Green Transition Fund' that would retrain and support people in the traditional automotive sector. It was a classic case of turning potential obstacles into opportunities, proving even the hairiest of challenges could be tackled with creativity and earnest effort.

Legislative Legacy

As our story of policy and regulation concludes, the government's role in promoting electric cars can be called both crucial and transformative. The policies hammered out in the hallways of Politicstown have set the stage for a cleaner, greener future, and their influence has been deeply felt, far and wide.

In the end, the story of electric vehicle policies is one of collaboration, innovation, and a bit of whimsical mechanical clockwork. Whether it be tax rebates or charging infrastructure, these policies have been chiseling out the electric car revolution and proving that even in legislation, sound economics and oodles of heart can make all the difference.

As we move forward, let us acknowledge the often overlooked policymakers who have shaped the landscape of this industry and waved their magic wand of incentives in laying the road for the new era of transportation. Their efforts remind us that even in the world of politics, the quest for a better world can be a story well-told.

Incentives and Economic Consequences for Inflation

Within the bustling city of Statistonia, policymakers crafted a sophisticated framework of economic incentives. The objective: to make electric cars more attractive while containing inflationary pressures.

Think of a vast alchemist's laboratory, bustling with lawmakers stirring cauldrons of tax credits, rebates, and subsidies while evading the "Inflation Gremlin" lurking in a dark corner.

Statistonia's government was very keen on promoting green technology and thus introduced a host of incentives. These included generous tax rebates for electric car buyers, subsidies to manufacturers with the aim of reducing production costs, and even grants for research into new battery technologies. This, in essence, sought to make electric vehicles not only a sustainable choice but also economically savvy.

However, as with any policy intervention, there were unintended consequences. The rapid increase in demand for electric vehicles, caused by their incentivized underlayment, triggered a wave of demand that had inflationary consequences for the economy. Armed with calculators and spreadsheets, the city's economic ministers began to observe a strange phenomenon: the price of raw materials for EV batteries was starting to rise (Mehdi & Moerenhout, 2023)[5].

The Fable of Inflation

In Statistonia, the escalating demand for electric vehicles gave rise to an uptick in the prices of critical battery components, such as lithium and cobalt. This cause and effect mirrors the economic principle of supply and demand, where increased demand for a scarce resource can lead to a corresponding rise in price.

The situation spurred the most vibrant debate among economists. "We've brewed up a storm," they joked, "and now we've got to navigate the fog of inflation." The challenge was in maintaining the balance between the allure of economic incentives and the rising costs that seemed threatening to leak into an across-the-board rise in prices. Amidst this uncertainty, economists turned to the major online book retailer to purchase 'Chart Your Own Path: A Workbook for Economic Data Visualization,' to equip themselves with the essential tools to tackle the complexities of grasping everyday economics. This workbook, with its practical templates and exercises, empowered the researchers and students to create compelling and informative visualizations that can shed light on complex economic trends.

In response to the rising demand for electric vehicles and the subsequent price surges in battery raw materials, the Statistonian leadership implemented a multifaceted approach. By carefully monitoring market conditions and adjusting incentives as needed, they sought to mitigate inflationary pressures. Additionally, they invested in initiatives to promote battery recycling and explore alternative materials, thereby diversifying the supply chain and reducing reliance on scarce resources. This delicate balancing act, required a combination of foresight, malleability, and maintaining economic fidelity.

Quirks of the Market

But for its neighbor, Prosperium, the effect of economic incentives on inflation played out differently. Prosperium had adopted electric cars with gusto, establishing a set of policies to make EVs the rule. Soon, the city's streets were buzzing with shiny new electric cars, and government incentives were credited with a big uptick in adoption.

But with the rise in popularity came also some of the more humorous peculiarities in the market. In response to such high demand for EVs, local dealerships began to sell "deluxe" versions of their regular EVs (Hardman, Fleming, Khare, & Ramadan, 2021)[6]. These were adorned with all sorts of features of luxury, from leather seats to custom paint jobs.

The price tags, however, resembled those seen more often in a high-end boutique than in the car dealership.

The result? A curious phenomenon where the average price of electric vehicles soared, along with the inflation rates of the city. And the citizens of Prosperium find themselves facing a certain paradox: While consumers may opt for electric vehicles to reduce their environmental impact, the premium associated with these vehicles can raise questions about the true cost of ownership (Edmunds, 2023)[7].

The Balancing Act

The story of economic incentives and inflation is not just one about statistics and policies; it is also about harmony - a complex balance of supply, demand, and economic consequence. The key thing is finding that balance in the benefits of incentives with the broader effects on the economy.

First, the remedy lay in the combination of innovation in policy and proactive measures inside our allegorical town - Statistonia. Dynamic adjustments of incentives by the government, considering current real-time economic data so as not to stroke the fires of inflation too aggressively, were introduced. They also invested in educational campaigns that would help consumers understand the long-term benefits of their choices, even when those short-term costs may seem higher (CleanTechnica, 2019)[8].

In Prosperium, the idea was to create competition for innovation among the manufacturers. By creating a fertile ground where new technologies and advanced materials would thrive, the city hoped to take off some of the inflationary pressures while keeping on schedule with the electric vehicle revolution.

The Moral of the Tale

As we reach the end of our visit to Prosperium, it's clear that the story of economic incentives and their impact on inflation is one of balance and foresight. Governmental policies do indeed play a very significant role in setting the course for electric vehicle revolution, but this is balanced with great attention towards the wider economic setting.

It is within the big picture of electric cars that incentives are heroes, while inflation is a tricky antagonist, one requiring very delicate management.

Through considerate policies and creative solutions, it is actually possible to keep this delicate dance in balance and see to it that this journey towards a greener future keep being economically and ecologically viable (Shapiro & Walker, 2022)[9]. By carefully considering the specific context and balancing the need for market-driven innovation with the importance of environmental stewardship, policymakers can develop effective strategies that promote both economic growth and sustainability.

And with the electric vehicle future ahead, let us remember what lessons Statistonia and Prosperium have to give. The path towards a greener economy is undoubtedly paved with challenges, but a combination of a lot of research-backed common sense and wit will lead us through the economic incentives and inflationary pressures we are forced to navigate, thus bringing us to a sustainable epoch in a smooth transition.

This study examines the role of government tax incentives impacting the adoption of electric vehicles in the United States[1].

1: Javadnejad, F., Jahanbakh, M., Pinto, C. A., & Saeidi, A. (2023). Analyzing incentives and barriers to electric vehicle adoption in the United States. Environment Systems and Decisions, 44(575-606). https://doi.org/10.1007/s10669-023-09958-3

This is an article about the challenges of building electric vehicle charging infrastructure in rural area[2].

2: U.S. Department of Transportation. (n.d.). Charging forward: A toolkit for planning and funding rural electric mobility infrastructure.

https://www.transportation.gov/rural/ev/toolkit

This paper analyzes the economics of electric vehicles and argues that government intervention is needed to promote their adoption[3].

3: Rapson, D. S., & Muehlegger, E. (2021). The economics of electric vehicles. National Bureau of Economic Research. https://www.nber.org/papers/w29093

This resource details the U.S. government's economic strategies and policies aimed at facilitating the shift to electric vehicles[4].

4: The Climate Group. (2021). Key policies to drive the electric vehicle transition in the US. https://www.theclimategroup.org/our-work/publications/key-policies-drive-electric-vehicle-transition-us

This study analyzes how government incentives have shaped the U.S. battery supply chain, leading to increased costs of raw materials essential for electric vehicle production[5].

5: Mehdi, A., & Moerenhout, T. (2023). The IRA and the US battery supply chain: Background and key drivers. Columbia University Center on Global Energy Policy. https://www.energypolicy.columbia.edu/publications/the-ira-and-the-us-battery-supply-chain-one-year-on/

This article provides an analysis of the integration of luxury electric vehicles into the market and the transition towards electric vehicle adoption[6].

6: Hardman, S., Fleming, K. L., Khare, E., & Ramadan, M. M. (2021). A perspective on equity in the transition to electric vehicles. MIT Science Policy Review.

https://sciencepolicyreview.org/2021/08/equity-transition-electric-vehicles/

This is a comparison of electric and internal combustion engine vehicles life cycle environmental impact and total cost of ownership[7].

7: Edmunds, T. (2023). Life Cycle Analysis Comparison: Electric and Internal Combustion Engine Vehicles. Transportation Energy Institute.

https://www.transportationenergy.org/research/reports/life-cycle-analysis-comparison-electric-and-internlife-cycle-analysis-comparison-electric-and-intern

According to the article, educating the masses is a critical step to overcome the barriers that hinder wider adoption of electric vehicles[8].

8: CleanTechnica. (2019, March 31). If We Want To See More EV Adoption, We Need To Educate The Masses. https://cleantechnica.com/2019/03/31/if-we-want-to-see-more-ev-adoption-we-need-to-educate-the-masses/

This article discusses how government policies can support both economic growth and environmental protection through strategic incentives[9].

9:Shapiro, J. S., & Walker, R. (2022). US Environmental Policies, the Environment, and the Economy. National Bureau of Economic Research.
https://www.nber.org/reporter/2022number2/us-environmental-policies-environment-and-economy

CHAPTER 6:

POLICY AND ECONOMIC OUTCOMES

In the grand narrative of the electric vehicle revolution, at the macroeconomics level, policy initiatives serve as the roadmap guiding this transition toward a sustainable future: the saga of the future of cars. The fundamental question that arises is how to judge their outcomes. How can we judge the worth of policy initiatives set in place to quicken electric car adoption? This chapter investigates the subtleties of economic indicators and quantitative research to explain policy effects on the economy, combined with a touch of allegory.

Studies Linking Policy Changes to Economic Outcomes

Under the free hand of the market, the District of Free Markets prospered. Within notebooks overflowing with datasets and analytics, merchants gleefully traded their products and services. The people of the land donned their spectacles prone to sliding down their noses, as they peered at the fleet of traditional combustible vehicles. They were poised to stand in judgement of the debate over the viability of electric vehicles, and the torrid affair between government acts and the electric vehicle revolution.

Other lands greeted electric vehicles as an aid in easing environmental sustainability concerns. In the laissez-faire paradise of the District of Free Markets, however, they began to research whether this claim needed thorough scrutiny and evaluation. They considered that promoting electric vehicle ownership would amount to a great deal of government intervention, making it inevitable that regulatory policy would inadvertently cause prices to go up and market distortions to result (Allcott & Greenstone, 2019)[1]. As questions arise about EV incentives' ability to last, so too does the sustained desirability of EVs. An in-depth look at the hidden costs of electric vehicles encompasses hidden costs which include environmental costs from lithium extraction and possible power system overload in response to increased charging requirements, as well as questions around battery disposal (Lee & Popp, 2021)[2].

Current regulations and policy changes add to these unintended consequences, on top of subsidizing electric vehicle manufacturing. Then the question of ecological principles arises: are not electric vehicles an essential advance toward a sustainable future? Should not the government encourage cleaner forms of transportation? Such methods have traditionally selected and given favor to producing large cars with long range batteries - a strategy which may ultimately cost more than smaller, more efficient cars. This raises doubts about the genuine advantages of EVs and whether they really are an improvement over traditional vehicles (Holland, Mansur, Muller, & Yates, 2015)[3].

There were proposals to mandate a bidirectional charging port that can push power back onto the grid, aiding to reduce the over surge of consumption on the power companies - two-way electric car chargers that can return power to the grid(U.S. Department of Energy, 2021)[4]. The people of the District of Free Markets felt as though while this regulation may appear to address a concern, it poses an overreach of government authority that is totally unnecessary. They feel that individuals' usage of electric vehicles, and its resulting surge in electricity use will force private enterprises into renewable energy sources for competition's sake (Rapson & Muehlegger, 2021)[5].

The victory of the District of Free Markets' free-market environmentalists with their clearly defined property rights and few regulations, produced acceptable environmental results. Where the people had their own, clearly defined property rights, they sought to ensure the longevity of their environment. In order to prevent unintended economic and environmental consequences, the transition to EV should be carefully managed to lend towards the greatest chance for sustainability.

The road to tomorrow will be a green one requiring a well-functioning GPS navigation to follow. While it is certainly true that market-based solutions have their merit, the role of government policies in the deliberate transition to electric cars cannot be underestimated. If we understand the economic effects and look at problems, this critical change can be navigated successfully - an essentially important step for the adoption of electric vehicles. The next step in evolution is now just ahead of us.

The electric vehicle revolution involves more than simply technology. It also reflects an intricate blend of economic incentives, infrastructure development and human behavior. Yet by thinking through these different issues thoroughly we can create a tomorrow in which the concept of clean transportation is not only conceivable but a well-accepted reality.

The Quest for Knowledge

As we visited the District of Free Markets' and their unseen hand of the market, approach to electric car adoption versus government involvement, the proportionate role that policy might play in accelerating change to electric vehicles is too crucial. And so, as we journey into the next land we'll see where policy, when carefully contrived, can bring about a steady change in both economic results and EV adoption.

Our story begins in the hallowed halls of Academia, where researchers and analysts pour over tomes of information and weave intricate tapestries of statistical analysis. The goal being to determine how different policies influence economic outcomes - particularly those involving electric vehicles.

The land was renowned for ambitious EV policies. The rulers introduced a host of incentives: tax rebates, subsidies to manufacturers, and investments in charging infrastructure.

With a little more than a collection of spreadsheets and a dedication to their quest rivaled by few, the scholars set out to measure the impact of these policies.

Indeed, the study found that Electra's policies had yielded a stunning effect on EV adoption: lured by generous rebates, the citizens flocked to the car dealerships to purchase their very own electric chariots. Soon enough, an astonishing array of eco-friendly vehicles lined the roads of the kingdom, and the air became remarkably cleaner though the sporadic waft of roasted marshmallows emanated from the land's new charging stations, it did indeed provide a curious aroma.

The Story of the Charging Infrastructure

Now, Academia invested greatly in its charging infrastructure. The government created a very widespread network of charging stations-from the busiest city center up to remote village squares. Its ambitious plan was to have the charging as easy to find as a tavern on Friday night.

Researchers with their power data collectors, were quick to set out and find out just how this investment was affecting the kingdom's economy.

Amazingly, the study revealed that the charging infrastructure increased the rates of EV adoption, and indeed, it had a spillover effect on local businesses.

Charging stations were becoming popular spots for bookshops, cafes, and even pet grooming services.

But there were too many; the charging stations were like lighthouse towers on a foggy night, guiding in entrepreneurs and rejuvenating local economies.

However, here is the cincher: the research also uncovered that charging stations had inadvertently become the most popular social spots in town.

People would just hang out at the charging station, using the downtime to gossip or sip a latte. In short, an afternoon sojourn where, in fact, the activity took all of five minutes. Voilà, 'charging social' entered the local vernacular, while Academia's coffee shops rejoiced. As the trend caught on, residents of Academia began seeking out ways to make these charging sessions more meaningful. Many turned to the large online book retailer to purchase the manual on building community through book clubs. The residents all bought a copy of "Page Turners to Friends & Shelf Love:

Your Practical Guide to Building Relationships Through Forming a Book Club." Inspired by the book, they organized book clubs that met at a local coffee shops with plenty of charging stations. There, amidst the buzz of conversation and their cars charging, and the aroma of freshly brewed coffee, the fellow book club members found a new sense of connection and community.

Unraveling the Mystery of Economic Incentives

The marvel of Academia with their research-backed decision making, which also introduced a package of economic incentives with a view to stimulating EV adoption. The incentives involved subsidies for EV manufacturers and a reduced sales tax on buyers.

This, showed a curious paradox. The incentives did indeed help sell more EVs, but as an unintended consequence of it all, some of the models started having slightly higher prices (Perkis, 2021)[6]. Supply and demand had played their part in forcing the prices up; consequently, there was a little grumbling from the populace. "It's the price of progress." they joked, though many hoped their next EV purchase would come with further discounts.

The people look forward to one important advantage, long-term financial benefits. The price increases during the first years were compensated for by savings on fuel and maintenance in subsequent years, eventually turning EVs more financially viable (Consumer Reports, 2020)[7].

In this respect, Academia's policy makers came to a conclusion that incentives might create short-term volatility in prices, but more importantly, they would eventually lead to a sustainable and economical future.

The Legend of Balanced Policies

As our time in this enchanted realm winds down, we find that Academia is a land that has achieved a good balance in its EV policies based on sound economic principles and solid research. The government struck a thoughtful balance of incentives, market forces, investments in infrastructure, and regulatory actions that would help the fostering of a vibrant EV market, controlling its economic impacts.

As a result of such balanced policies, Academia found a narrative of harmony therein. The kingdom found itself with high EV adoption rates, a thriving local economy, and contained inflation.

It seems that success lies in balancing policy measures to support short-term adoption and long-term stability (Zaino, 2021)[8].

Academia's approach was described as 'the Goldilocks solution', as it wasn't too regulated nor too unregulated; but just right. For this kingdom's citizens, who continued to use the name with mirth, an apparent reflective balance had gone into the decision making, and they were reaping the positive effects on their lives.

Moral of the Story

As we conclude our chapter, what stands out is that the story of policy changes and their economic outcomes are indeed a well-crafted and insightfully analyzed tale. Tales from the District of Free Markets, Electra, and Academia demonstrate that well-crafted policies can yield large-scale benefits, from accelerated EV adoption to the revitalization of local economies.

More importantly, the journey underlines how a policy needs continuous monitoring and adaptation in case unwanted side effects arise. The intricate narrative arc of the folktale serves as a poignant metaphor, illustrating that while policies have the potential to yield remarkable results, their efficacy hinges upon meticulous management to secure favorable and sustainable outcomes.

This analysis reveals that federal subsidies for electric vehicles have increased adoption, though their distributional impact warrants further scrutiny[1].
1: Allcott, H., & Greenstone, M. (2019). Assessing Federal Subsidies for Purchases of Electric Vehicles. National Bureau of Economic Research.
https://www.nber.org/digest/jun19/assessing-federal-subsidies-purchases-electric-vehicles

This study on electric vehicle adoption, economic competitiveness hinges on further battery cost reduction and charging infrastructure improvements[2].
2: Lee, K., & Popp, D. (2021). Charging the Future: Challenges and Opportunities for Electric Vehicle Adoption. Harvard Energy Policy Group.
https://projects.iq.harvard.edu/files/energyconsortium/files/rwp18-026_lee_1.pdf

An analysis of whether electric vehicles have a positive or negative impact on the environment, and whether subsidies for electric vehicles are cost-effective[3].
3: Holland, S. P., Mansur, E. T., Muller, N. Z., & Yates, A. J. (2015). Environmental Benefits from Driving Electric Vehicles? National Bureau of Economic Research.
https://www.nber.org/papers/w21291

This article discusses investments in electric vehicle infrastructure, integrating renewable energy solutions and optimizing grid efficiency[4].
4: U.S. Department of Energy. (2021). Biden-Harris Administration Announces New Private and Public Sector Investments for Affordable Electric Vehicles.

https://www.whitehouse.gov/briefing-room/statements-releases/2021/04/17/fact-sheet-biden-harris-administration-announces-new-private-and-public-sector-investments-for-affordable-electric-vehicles/

This paper discusses the private and public economics of electric vehicles, including the role of market forces and incentives[5].
5: Rapson, D. S., & Muehlegger, E. (2021). The Economics of Electric Vehicles. National Bureau of Economic Research. https://www.nber.org/papers/w29093

Article on how supply and demand dynamics fundamentally shape market prices, influencing economic equilibrium[6].
6: Perkis, D. F. (2021). The Science of Supply and Demand. Federal Reserve Bank of St. Louis. https://www.stlouisfed.org/publications/page-one-economics/2021/03/01/the-science-of-supply-and-demand

This source discusses how electric vehicle adoption leads to substantial long-term consumer savings by eliminating fuel expenses[7].
7: Consumer Reports. (2020). EVs Offer Big Savings Over Traditional Gas-Powered Cars. https://www.consumerreports.org/hybrids-evs/evs-offer-big-savings-over-traditional-gas-powered-cars/

This review explores strategic policy integration is key to fostering both immediate electric vehicle adoption and ensuring long-term market resilience[8].
8: Zaino, R. (2021). Electric Vehicle Adoption: A Comprehensive Systematic Review of Technological, Environmental, Organizational and Policy Impacts. MDPI. https://www.mdpi.com/2032-6653/15/8/375

CONCLUSION

Throughout this electrifying saga of electric vehicles and how they are affecting inflation, we are standing at the crossroads of reflection and foresight.

The story we have traveled is not about cars and economics; it's about innovation, policy, and how those two dance with the ever-changing global markets.

Let us recapitulate the core findings and revisit the salient points and ponder the trajectory of our inquiry.

We started our journey with the rise of electric vehicles, tracing it from a niche novelty to a mainstream marvel.

From pioneering times to today's bustling markets, electric cars are sparking revolutions in transport, cleaner air and eco-sustainability for the future.

The story has taken us through the historical setting, technological strides, and shifting sands of consumer adoption.

The deeper we swam through the sea of economic principles and this elaborate inflationary dance, the more eccentricities and enigmas this green revolution met.

With the rising EVs came a rollercoaster of economic effects from rising raw material prices to an inflationary seesaw of incentives.

The saga of economic incentives revealed a rich tale of both victories and setbacks, reinforcing the timeless principle that even the most well-intentioned policies can produce unintended outcomes. In this, research offers insight into real-world effects this electric vehicle boom created.

From the bright success story of Electra to the social charging phenomenon happening in Academia, each tale flowed differently to tell the story of how shifts in policies ripple through economies, illustrating varied outcomes from similar regions.

This revolution brought a whole new psychological and social dimension in our narration.

We saw the shift of public perception, consumer behavioral changes, altered hopes, and hesitations while the adoption of electric vehicles unraveled a society in transition.

Changes happening in social dynamics were proof that technological development impinges on our daily lives.

As we explored policies and regulations, we saw how each land had used its authority to affect the direction of electric cars. Some of the many policies that have helped put the electric vehicle revolution on track include subsidies and infrastructure investments (McKinsey & Company, 2020)[1]. But as our story demonstrated, it is not a road without bumps and twists, one that treads an uneasy balance between progress and economic stability.

The Way Forward

In conclusion, it's clear that the electric vehicle revolution will continue for the foreseeable future. There are numerous possibilities, challenges, and opportunities on the horizon. The insights we've gained from our exploration can guide us through the complex landscape of technological innovation and its economic impact.

The future of electric vehicles is bright, with endless possibilities for greater technological advancement, rapid diffusion, and a constant struggle to minimize the negative impacts of inflation and economic disruption that we see today. As policymakers, businesses, and consumers plot out this roadmap, our experiences will be critical building blocks in our quest to create a sustainable and prosperous future.

The electric vehicle revolution is not a story of cars but more so a general tale of human ingenuity, of economic adaptation, and a quest for a cleaner world. It's a reminder that every innovation carries with it the potential for profound change, both positive and challenging.

Final Thoughts and Call to Action

And so, as we close the pages of this saga, may that spirit remain with us in continued curiosity and optimism.

The electric vehicle journey is one example of what can be achieved when innovation meets determination.

This journey shares its roadmap through economically complex times of change. Ultimately, our story is less about the past and more about the future. It is the way that policymakers, business leaders, and everyday consumers will go together toward a greener, more sustainable world. By learning from the lessons on our journey and embracing the opportunities of the path ahead, we may contribute to a future in which progress and prosperity come hand in glove.

As we move further up the road into the horizon, let us keep our eyes on the road, our hearts in the right place, and our minds open toward possibilities that are well within sight. The adventure is far from over, and with each mile traveled, we move closer to a world where innovation continues to fuel not just economic growth but a brighter future as well, a cleaner future for all.

This paper discusses the strategic financial incentives that have been pivotal in accelerating the widespread adoption of electric vehicles[1].

1: McKinsey & Company. (2020). Building the Electric Vehicle Charging Infrastructure America Needs.
https://www.mckinsey.com/industries/public-sector/our-insights/building-the-electric-vehicle-charging-infrastructure-america-needs

www.ingramcontent.com/pod-product-compliance
Lightning Source LLC
Chambersburg PA
CBHW020451220526
45464CB00002B/954